BEST PRACTICES FOR STARTING AND MANAGING A MORE SUCCESSFUL BUSINESS

CONTENTS

ACKNOWLEDGEMENTS

Special thanks to my wife, Bonisiwe, who has been supportive during the time when I was working on this book. Without you, I would not have done this effectively. Thanks also go to my daughter Nompumelelo and my son Melokuhle, who have been understanding and patient as I spent a lot of time working on the book.

FOREWORD

The agreement between idea and action is best described in the book. Ideas are worthless if there is no corresponding action, desire, or determination.

A man is born a natural entrepreneur. The Author creates from the beginning the foundational balance required to be successful, and embedded in it are principles of prosperity.

Ideas remain dormant if not worked out, and precision of action, as detailed by the author, is fundamental to the achievement of any set goals or targets.

It's marvelous to note the interaction between the thought process and the practical implementation. Basic financial principles are outlined in relation to stage and business cycle.

The author has tremendously answered the "how to start" question that is a stumbling block for most entrepreneurs. This is a display of wisdom and grace at work in the life of Reverend Elphas Sipho Mdluli.

Salutations are in order
Phesheya Andile Zwane

INTRODUCTION

Every normal individual has a dream. Most dreams start in childhood. As one grows, some dreams drop, but some grow with the individual. Dreams differ by individual. That is a sign that we are different. Each individual has dreams about different things that pertain to his life. Some of our dreams are shaped by the environment we are exposed to. One dreams of a good family, a career, and other great endeavors.

When it comes to a career, some have dream jobs. Others want to start their own businesses to earn a living. They want to make money by themselves and be independent. This book is all about starting and managing the profitable business of your dreams. In order for one to fulfill his dream of starting such a business, there are some things he needs to learn. These things include understanding what is meant by entrepreneurship. Furthermore, he wants to know important tips for starting a profitable business.

Every successful endeavor in life starts with a dream. Then there is an idea of how the dream can be fulfilled. Once the entrepreneur has interacted with the idea, there will be opportunities. Opportunities must find you prepared to take advantage of them. If you are not ready, then it is not an opportunity for you but will remain an idea.

A profitable business involves a plan for the future. There have to be goals and objectives set for the business. Once these goals have been set and the plan is complete, management is needed to implement the plan for the business. There are skills required for this. You will be dealing with people who will assist in ensuring that your plan is implemented. There will be a need for customers, without whom there can be no business. There must be a plan on how to get customers.

Once the customers have come, it should be everyone's duty to treat them well in the business. Otherwise, you can sell to them once. That can lead to high costs and expenses for getting new customers. Offer them a great service so they can come back. Customers are a valuable asset for any business.

This book will therefore be like a manual for effectively starting and managing your business. By so doing, you will realize your precious dream of making money through your business. You will also realize the benefits of becoming an independent entrepreneur. So let us dive in and get started on your beautiful journey.

CHAPTER 1: ENTREPRENEURSHIP

To any entrepreneur: if you want to do it, do it now. If you don't, you're going to regret it. - Catherine Cook, co-founder of MyYearbook.

For it will be like a man going on a journey, who called his servants and entrusted to them his property. To one he gave five talents, to another two, to another one, to each according to his ability. Then he went away. He who had received the five talents went at once and traded with them, and he made five talents more. So also he who had the two talents made two talents more. But he who had received the one talent went and dug in the ground and hid his master's money... (Matthew 25:14-30 ESV).

Do you see a man skillful in his work? He will stand before kings; he will not stand before obscure men. (Proverbs 22:29 ESV).

Bread is made for laughter, and wine gladdens life, and money answers everything. (Ecclesiastes 10:19 ESV).

God created us to be industrial. We were meant to be productive and creative in life. He expected us to create or make value to benefit humanity as a whole. So entrepreneurship is Biblical. God is not opposed to making money. Making money requires entrepreneurship.

In order for anything new or old to be improved for the benefit of humanity and life, there has to be entrepreneurship. This is important whether or not we talk of an invention in any area of life. It may be in science, business, the economy, education, spirituality, etc. Any invention in life involves entrepreneurship.

What is entrepreneurship?

One cannot talk about starting a business without talking about entrepreneurship. There are different definitions of an entrepreneur.

Entrepreneurship is the process of creating something different and valuable by devoting the necessary time and effort, assuming the accompanying financial, psychological, and social risks, and receiving the resulting rewards of monetary and personal satisfaction, according to Bowen and Hisrich (1986).

According to Scarborough (2012:4), an entrepreneur is one who creates a new business in the face of risk and uncertainty for the purpose of achieving profit and growth by identifying opportunities and assembling the necessary resources to capitalize on those opportunities.

Holt (1992:7) defines entrepreneurship as the dynamic process of creating incremental wealth. Individuals create this wealth by assuming the major risks in terms of equity, time, and/or career commitment of providing value for some product or service. So the product or service may either be new or not. However, somehow there must be added value for the entrepreneur as he secures and allocates the required resources and skills.

Bateman and Snell (1996:208) define it as "the act of forming a new organization of value". It is the seemingly discontinuous process of combining resources to produce new goods or services.

Many simply equate it with starting one's own business. However, most economists believe it is more than that. According to some economists, an entrepreneur is someone who is willing to bear the risk of a new venture if there is a significant chance for profit. Others emphasize the entrepreneur's role as an innovator who markets his innovation. Still others say that entrepreneurs develop new goods or processes that the market demands but is not currently supplied with.

What are the benefits of entrepreneurship?

According to Zimmer and Scarborough (2005:6), the benefits of entrepreneurship are as follows:

1) Opportunity to create your own destiny
As an entrepreneur, you attain independence as well as the opportunity to achieve what is important to you. It must be stated, however, that this requires effort.

2) You have an opportunity to make a difference.
You combine your concerns for social issues with the desire to earn a good living. Impacting your communities in a great way is possible as you meet the needs of your society.

3) Opportunity to reach your full potential
As an entrepreneur, you can use your business as an instrument for self-expression and self-actualization. You can do what you enjoy doing. Your dreams are unlimited. You are the only one who can limit your business's potential.

4) You can reap impressive profits.
The motivation of an entrepreneur is the potential to earn profits. As long as you are able to add value and reduce costs as much as possible in your business, you can earn good profits.

5) Contribution to society and recognition for your effort
As an entrepreneur, you have the opportunity to contribute to society. The good thing is that as you contribute to society, your efforts are rewarded. Earning money is about identifying what people need. If you meet a need, people will gladly give money to

you. It is an exchange where there is value that can be appreciated.

How does one see an entrepreneur?

1) Prepared to take risks
2) Driven by achievement
3) Not put off by failure (e.g., Edison)
4) Self-motivated
5) Determined to stay ahead of the competition

What are the challenges of entrepreneurship?

Entrepreneurship is great. As much as there are many benefits, there are also challenges or drawbacks associated with them. Here are some of the disadvantages and financial risks of entrepreneurship:

1) Uncertainty of income
2) The risk of losing your entire investment or capital
3) Long hours and hard work
4) Decreased or lower quality of life until the business gets established
5) Complete responsibility
6) Reputation and self-confidence

Deadly mistakes of entrepreneurship

Mistakes should not be viewed in a bad light. No human being is immune to making mistakes. We just need to view them from a good perspective. The good thing about mistakes is that we learn from them. At times, they offer the best lesson, which we cannot forget easily.

One of the reasons our children do not learn valuable lessons is that we teach them to be afraid and shun mistakes. But when you look at great entrepreneurs who are successful, you find that they made a lot of mistakes. The following are some of the mistakes that are deadly:

1) Management mistakes
2) Lack of experience
3) Poor financial controls
4) Weak marketing efforts
5) Failure to develop a strategic plan
6) Uncontrolled growth
7) Poor location
8) Improper inventory control
9) Incorrect pricing
10) Inability to make the entrepreneurial transition

The importance of entrepreneurship in Small businesses

Small businesses are vital to the success of an economy. This is not just about providing success stories for the future; it also meets local needs. Examples may include Hairdressers, financial consultants, emergency plumbers, etc.

They serve the requirements of larger businesses, e.g., Photography services, printed stationary, catering, and routine maintenance.

CHAPTER 2: BUSINESS

Making money is art and working is art and good business is the best art- Andy Warhol.

What is business?

> *You shall remember the Lord your God, for it is he who gives you power to get wealth, that he may confirm his covenant that he swore to your fathers, as it is this day.(Deuteronomy 8:18 ESV).*

> *And if you make a sale to your neighbor or buy from your neighbor, you shall not wrong one another. (Leviticus 25:14 ESV).*

> *For even when we were with you, we would give you this command: If anyone is not willing to work, let him not eat. (2 Thessalonians 3:10 ESV).*

There is a need to do business. We can note from the above portions of scripture that we are expected to trade. Making money through business is found in the Bible. God has granted us the ability to engage in business. Business creates opportunities for others to be employed so as to contribute to the economy of a community or country.

Let us now define business:

CISP (2014:44) defines business as any activity that adds value to life or enhances survival. If you are in business, it means you are providing goods or services. It does not matter the size or nature of the business; the important thing is whether the business makes profit, creates value, or helps its owner live a better life. A business may be small, medium, or large.

The Business Dictionary (2017) defines business as an organization or economic system where goods and services are exchanged for one another or for money. Every business requires some form of investment and enough customers to whom its output can be sold on a consistent basis in order to make a profit. Businesses can be privately owned, not-for-profit, or state-owned. An example of a corporate business is PepsiCo, while a mom-and-pop catering business is a private enterprise.

Investopedia defines business as an organization or enterprising entity engaged in commercial, industrial, or professional activities. A company transacts business activities through the production of a good, the offering of a service, or the retailing of already manufactured products. A business can be a for-profit entity or a nonprofit organization that operates to fulfill a charitable mission.

The main types of business

There are four types of businesses:
1) Manufacturing
2) Wholesale
3) Retail
4) Service

Manufacturing business

A manufacturing business is any business that uses

components, parts, or raw materials to make a finished good. These finished goods can be sold directly to consumers or to other manufacturing businesses that use them to make a different product. Manufacturing businesses in today's world are normally comprised of machines, robots, computers, and humans that all work in a specific manner to create a product.

Manufacturing plants often use an assembly line, which is a process where a product is put together in sequence from one work station to the next. By moving the product down an assembly line, the finished product can be put together quicker with less manual labor. It's important to note that some industries refer to the manufacturing process as fabrication.

Manufacturing businesses can be very simple, with only a few parts required for assembly, or they can be very complicated, with hundreds of parts needed to create a finished product. Compared to other businesses, manufacturing businesses usually have more legal regulations and environmental laws to deal with. These things can range from scrutinized labor laws to environmental and pollution issues. Although labor unions are not as common as they were 50 years ago, they still exist heavily in the manufacturing industry, where wages, benefits, and other rights are negotiated. Let's take a look at a few examples of manufacturing businesses.

An example of a manufacturing business is Ford. Ford is one of the largest U.S.-based automakers and has been manufacturing vehicles on a large scale since the early 1900s. The assembly lines are a great visual for what a manufacturing business does. Ford can easily make over five million cars in a single year!

Wholesale business

Wholesaling, jobbing, or distributing is the sale of goods or merchandise to retailers; to industrial, commercial, institutional, or other professional business users; or to other wholesalers and related subordinated services. In general, it is the sale of goods to anyone other than a standard consumer.

According to the Investopedia Dictionary, wholesaling is the sale and distribution of goods to specific customer types, such as those most commonly referred to as resellers. Resellers are traditionally retailers, other wholesalers, or merchants who will resell the goods to an end user. Certain industrial, commercial, and institutional customers also qualify, as the goods are often components of a different end product.

Wholesaling often occurs when large quantities of merchandise are purchased in bulk with the intent of reassembling, sorting, repackaging, or distributing the goods in smaller lots. Due to the volume of the purchase, the price of the goods is often lower than the price offered to retail consumers. A wholesaler can also be a business that acts as a middleman, brokering deals between businesses that produce certain components that are not intended for immediate sale on the open market.

Retail business

A business or person that sells goods to the consumer, as opposed to a wholesaler or supplier, who normally sell their goods to another business, according to the Business Dictionary.

If you are a retailer, then you need to make sure that your

product is great and that you are marketing it as best as you can.

Service business

A commercial enterprise that provides work performed in an expert manner by an individual or team for the benefit of its customers. The typical service business provides intangible products such as accounting, banking, consulting, cleaning, landscaping, education, insurance, treatment, and transportation services.

According to the Business Dictionary, a service business is a commercial enterprise that provides work performed in an expert manner by an individual or team for the benefit of its customers. The typical service business provides intangible products such as accounting, banking, consulting, cleaning, landscaping, education, insurance, treatment, and transportation services.

Forms of business

Under the main forms of business, we have the following:

1) Sole proprietorship
2) Partnership
3) Company
4) Close Corporation

Knowing the legal forms of business organization will help you choose which one will be suitable for your business as an entrepreneur. This will depend on the benefits you want to enjoy from it and the long-term prospects you desire.

Firer et al. (2012:4-6) highlight four legal forms of business organization. These are sole proprietorships, partnerships, companies, and close corporations. When you start your own business, you may choose from these forms. They are described as follows:

Sole proprietorship

One person is the owner of this company. This is the simplest business one can start. It is the least regulated. It is the least expensive to establish (CISP, 2014:47). You get a trading license, and then you can have your doors open for business. Some large companies started out as small proprietorships.

As the owner of such a business, you keep all the profits for yourself. But you have unlimited liability for the debts caused by your sole proprietorship business. The income you get from this business is taxed as personal income. Capital is often limited since you are unable to borrow from financial institutions as a business. You borrow money in your personal capacity, which is difficult most of the time. A sole proprietor can therefore raise capital from personal savings or borrow from friends and relatives. Ownership may be difficult to transfer.

Partnership

With the exception of the fact that there are between two and twenty partners, this structure is similar to a sole proprietorship. So these partners are owners. The partners share in both the losses and profits of the business. When it comes to the debts of the partnership business, the partners are all liable. There has to be a partnership agreement that stipulates each partner's responsibilities, how profits and losses will be divided, how a partner can leave the business, and what happens in cases of a partner's death, disability, or serious discord.

This agreement may be informal or formal. However, if the agreement is informal, there will be a problem when conflicts arise. The advantages and disadvantages are basically the same as those of a sole proprietorship. The capital raised is limited to the wealth of the partners. Transferring ownership is difficult since it would require the formation of a new partnership agreement. If a partner dies, the partnership has to be terminated. It is not easy to develop because acquiring capital is difficult because of the limitations that come with this formation.

Company

A company is sometimes called a corporation. This is a form of business that is distinctively created as a separate legal entity. It is considered a legal person and is separate from its owner(s). A company is composed of one or more individuals or entities. It has a number of rights, duties, and privileges. A company can own property, borrow money, enter into contracts, sue, and be sued.

A company is incorporated through the Companies Act of your country. A profit company is a company formed for the purpose of financial gain for the shareholders (owners). There is also a non-profit company that is solely formed for the public's benefit. This is a formation that is more complicated when compared to the other forms of businesses. There has to be a memorandum of understanding and articles of association among the required documentation.

Close Corporation

According to Firer (2012:6), there is a new legal form of corporate personality for small businesses that has been introduced in South Africa. It provides a much simpler and less expensive legal form for entrepreneurs or a few participants. At the same time, it retains the concept of a company as a legal person separate from its owners. Their existence may be terminated through deregistration, dissolution, or transfer to a private company under the Companies Act.

Small business versus big business

A small business is an independently owned and operated company that is limited in size and revenue depending on the industry, according to Yourdictionary (2016:1). It employs less than 500 employees for manufacturing companies.

The benefits of small business when compared with big business

Small businesses prosper and survive for the following reasons:

1) Developing personal relationships
Small businesses are well placed to build personal relationships with customers, employees, and suppliers. With a small business, you know who you are dealing with. You can "put a face" on the person you contact.

2) Flexibility in responding to problems and challenges

There is little hierarchy or chain of command in a small business. Large businesses may have set ways of operating and established procedures that are hard to change. Small businesses can reach decisions quicker than large ones.

3) Inventiveness and innovation

Small businesses are well positioned to introduce and develop new ideas. The owners do not have to report and seek approval somewhere else.

4) Low overheads

Since small businesses operate on a small scale, they have low overheads due to small premises, low heating and lighting costs, and limited rents and rates to pay. Lower prices result in lower prices for consumers.

5) Catering for a limited or niche market

Large firms with high overheads must produce high levels of output to spread costs. In contrast, small businesses are able to make a profit on much lower sales figures.

6) Small businesses give people independence.

They also reap the rewards themselves. Those are powerful incentives.

Disadvantages of small businesses compared to big ones

Small businesses have their disadvantages when compared to big businesses, and they are as follows:

1) It involves hard work and making most decisions on your own. There is little time for holidays initially. There are also considerable risks.

2) It is hard to find economies of scale from which big firms are able to benefit. Big firms get discounts, and it is not easy to raise finance.

CHAPTER 3: BUSINESS IDEAS AND EXPLOITING OPPORTUNITY

Twenty years from now, you will be more disappointed by the things that you didn't do than by the ones you did do, so throw off the bowlines, sail away from safe harbor, catch the trade winds in your sails. Explore, Dream, Discover. Mark Twain, author.

"Trust in the LORD with all your heart and lean not on your own understanding. In all thy ways acknowledge him and he shall direct all thy paths." (Proverbs 3: 5-6).

"Come let us reason together" says the LORD. 'If you be willing and obedient, you shall eat the fruit of the land." (Isaiah 1: 18-19).

Businesses start with an idea. This idea is then converted into a business plan if there is an opportunity in it.

What is a business idea?

According to Martins (2017), a business idea is a concept that can be used to make money. Usually, it centers on a product or service that can be offered for money. An idea is the first milestone in the process of founding a business. Every successful business starts with someone's idea. Although a business idea has the potential to make money, it initially has no commercial value. In fact, most business ideas exist in abstract form, usually in the mind of their creator or investor, and not all business ideas, no matter how brilliant they may seem, will end up being profitable. In order to find out about an idea's chances in the market and check its innovative content and feasibility, you need to conduct a plausibility check. Furthermore, Martins (2017) argues that a promising business idea must have the following characteristics:

1) Relevant (must fulfill customers' needs or solve their problems)
2) Innovative
3) Unique
4) Clear focus
5) Profitable in the long run

The acceptability and profitability of a business idea hinge largely on how innovative it is. Being innovative means using conventional production or distribution methods that have rarely been adopted before. In fact, the entire business system could be improved.

So starting your own business is a great idea for creating wealth. The creation of wealth is through business, not employment. Many of the richest people in the world are not employees but owners of businesses. Wealth creation is not related to education either. While education may help someone get a better grasp of issues, it is not usually a factor in the accumulation of business skills or acumen. Many businessmen who had humble beginnings at the local market have become rich businessmen who now own many businesses and properties. Business requires sheer hard work and the ability to identify profit-making opportunities. It is the ability to identify good business ideas that can propel a person to become a successful entrepreneur.

The size of the business idea is dependent on the ability and objective of the businessperson. A mother taking care of her children may think of the idea of selling home-cooked food in a kiosk at the livestock markets. Many mothers have done such business and educated their children through such very small businesses. Many ladies run stalls at the local markets and have been carrying out such business activities for many years. A business idea that is very profitable and satisfying to one person may not be so to another.

How to generate business ideas

The kind of business to start will depend on how the businessperson perceives the needs of the customers. Many people do business that is closely related to other existing businesses in the area. They do not look at the needs of the people; they just copy what already exists in an area and engage in it. The problem with such an approach is that it may lead to market saturation for the same kind of business.

The common businesses in this region are hotels, clothes, wholesale and retail shops and kiosks, livestock and livestock product sales, and pharmacies. Nowadays, private schools have also become commonplace. There are few consulting or knowledge-based businesses.

There are always businesses that you can start because everyone else is doing the same thing. You might have considered a stall or a shop selling clothes or livestock. While this is still not a bad idea, it is definitely harder to make money in an already crowded market. The problem with this idea is that there are already hundreds of people engaged in the same activity, which will reduce the market needed for the business to be successful. Starting a business based on a trend or copying what every other businessperson is engaged in can be a recipe for disaster. Instead, you should ask yourself the following five questions: The answers to these questions will be much more helpful than any list of hot businesses.

1) What is something that I do well that I like to do?

As in life, we tend to succeed and do well when we are engaged in something that we really enjoy. Your business should be no different. You may start a bakery because you like baking and can do it very well. You may start a tailoring shop because you think you can create stylish clothes and because you enjoy making and designing clothes. Do what you love, and the money will follow.

2) Is there a market for this business?

Let's say that the thing you love doing is running a barbershop and a salon. Well, there is no shortage of businesses that revolve around that concept, such as salons and barbershops. But what if the thing you love most is training bulls for a fight? There is likely to be very little interest in that initially. However interesting it may be to you, you don't have a business if no one is willing to pay you for your expertise. So you have to be realistic—there must be a market willing to buy what you want to sell.

3) Can I afford to start this business?

Some businesses are very inexpensive to start, most notably home-based businesses. Others can be quite expensive. In addition to picking a business that you like and for whom you have a market, you also must make sure that it is one you can afford to start.

4) What will distinguish my business?

Your business must offer something unique if you are to attract customers. After all, they already shop somewhere else. Why will they choose to buy from you? You must offer better quality, cheaper prices, a more convenient location, better service, and a unique product—something that makes you stand out from the crowd.

5) Can I make a profit?

Whatever business you start, whatever product or service you sell, you have to be able to sell it at a price high enough to make a profit, but low enough that people will buy it. Setting this price is not always an easy task. Why do so many stores and wholesalers go out of business? It is often because their overhead is too high, despite having a good product. Before jumping into a business, look at some numbers.

You need to look at the revenues and expenses of the business. Although all of these issues are important, they should point in one direction, namely, your passion. As you know, working with passion is one of the great joys of life. This is even truer when choosing a business. This business is going to become your baby. You will love it, care for it, nurse it along, and obsess over it. You will also be putting an extraordinary number of hours into it. You will be working at it all day, every day, hopefully for many years. Unless you love it deeply and are passionate about it, working so hard will be difficult.

Sources of business ideas

In order to get business ideas, you can consider the following:

1) People's needs and problems

This can be identified by observing the needs of people in a particular area. For example, an area that has a high concentration of shops and wholesalers may require transport.

2) Entrepreneur's talents and hobbies

This refers to the person's ability and what the person likes doing. For example, someone who likes cooking may start a catering business.

3) Entrepreneur's skills and experiences

This is the training of the entrepreneur and the ability to apply such training; an individual trained as a mechanic may start a vehicle repair garage, a mason may start a small construction company, and a trained waiter may start a hotel business.

4) Available resources

This means the various valuable items available in the environment that can be used to produce goods or services. For example, where there is a slaughterhouse, hides and skins can be obtained, tanned, and made into shoes and handbags.

5) Trends and fashion

This means the current wave of products on the market is selling fast. The kind of clothes, ornaments, or shoes that people like at a particular time is a source of business ideas.

The kind of business to start is dependent on the environment in which the businessperson lives. The business idea must take into consideration the culture and customs of the population. This does not mean the businessperson should not be creative; it just means that the businessperson should be careful not to engage in exotic ventures that may not be profitable in the end. A poultry farm, fattening young sheep for mutton production, pure leather shoe production, and a public bath system where customers are charged for using the baths and toilets. Online businesses have been introduced. You can engage in network and affiliate marketing.

The size of the business is dependent on the capital requirement. A housewife will be comfortable starting a house-call beauty business where she visits her lady customers at their homes for hair care and beautification. When the funds are available, she can convert her business into a walk-in beauty shop, and she can expand to several towns by hiring other ladies who can take care of her customers. She can then start her own cosmetic shops to supply her salons and also sell to the general public.

Not all business ideas will be successful. The businessperson must try many ideas and examine their success. Once one idea works, it can be used as a launch pad for many other businesses.

Deciding on an area that you love is only the first step when choosing a business to start. The rest of the required analysis is much more reasoned and analytical.

What is a business opportunity?

The race is neither to the swift, nor the battle to the strong, neither is bread to the wise, nor riches to men of understanding, nor favor to men of skill but time and chance happens to them all. (Ecclesiastes 9:11).

For whatsoever thy hands find to do, do it with all thy might; for there is no work, nor device, nor knowledge, nor wisdom in the grave. (Ecclesiastes 9:10).

But there are some things that you cannot be sure of. You must take a chance. If you wait for perfect weather, you will never plant your seeds. If you are afraid that every cloud will bring rain, you will never harvest your crops. (Ecclesiastes 11:4 ERV).

There are opportunities in life. These opportunities exist for both individuals and businesses. Scripture indicates that there are opportunities. Take advantage of a business opportunity. Normally, an opportunity does not wait for one forever. If not taken, it passes like time.

A business opportunity, according to Martins (2017), is a proven concept that generates on-going income. In other words, a business opportunity is a business idea that has been researched, refined, and packaged into a promising venture that is ready to launch.

While multiple business ideas may strike you on a daily basis, only a few of them will be profitable in the long run based on market research and feasibility studies conducted. These are the real business opportunities. An opportunity is regarded as one after it has been found to meet the following criteria:

1) It must have high gross margins.
2) It must have the potential to reach break-even cash flow within 12 to 36 months.
3) The startup capital investments must be realistic and within the range of what you can provide.
4) You must have the strength and ability needed to drive the business to success.
5) Your level of enthusiasm for the business must be very high.
   6) It must have the potential for residual income.
   7) It must have the potential to keep improving with time.
   8) It must have a low level of liability risk.

After you have refined and packaged your business opportunity in your mind, you can have it documented by writing a business plan. You can then either implement it on your own or sell it to someone else for profit (probably because you cannot afford the capital required to flag off the business).

When is a business idea a business opportunity?

A business idea can be an opportunity. But in order for it to be an opportunity, it must fulfill the following conditions:

1) Fill customers' needs
2) Have the skills and resources to start a business.
3) Be able to sell the product or service at a reasonable price and still profit.
4) Get your product or service to customers before the window of opportunity closes.
5) If you can keep the business going

The major functions of a business

These are very important things to do before the business starts operating. In other words, they can be referred to as requirements for starting to operate a formal business entity.

1) Planning

Business Plan: a detailed written statement that describes the nature of the business, target market, advantages the business will have over competition, resources, and owner qualifications. A business plan forces potential owners to be specific about what they will offer. A business plan is mandatory for talking with bankers or investors.

A good plan takes quality time to prepare. A good executive summary catches interest and tempts potential investors to read on. Getting the plan into the right hands is almost as important as getting the right information from it.

2) Financing

Sources of capital include personal savings, relatives, former employers, banks and finance companies, and venture capitalists —individuals or companies that invest in new businesses in exchange for partial ownership. The source of finance is key to the growth of a business entity. Limitations to raising sufficient capital will depend on the form of business organization you choose.

3) Knowing customers (The Market)

Market: This refers to consumers with unsatisfied wants and needs who have both resources and the willingness to buy.

Set out to fill the market's needs by offering top quality and great service at a fair price. One of the great advantages of small businesses is their ability to know the market and quickly adapt to its needs.

4) Managing employees

Hiring, training, and motivating employees are critical. Employees of small companies are often more satisfied with their jobs; they feel challenged and respected. Entrepreneurs best serve themselves and the business if they recruit and groom employees for management positions.

5) Keeping records

Computers simplify the process by helping with inventory control, customer records, and payroll. A good accountant can help in deciding whether to buy or lease equipment, whether to own or rent a building, tax planning, financial forecasting, choosing sources of financing, and writing requests for funds. This is discussed in detail in Chapter 7.

6) Legal Help

Business owners need outside consulting advice early in the process. Small and medium-sized firms cannot afford to hire experts as employees. A competent lawyer can help with the following:

1. Leases
2. Contracts
3. Partnership agreements
4. Protection against liabilities

7) Marketing Research

Marketing decisions need to be made long before introducing a product or opening a business. A marketing research study can help you determine where to locate, who to select as your target market, and what is an effective strategy for reaching the market. This has been covered in detail under Chapter 8.

8) Other Forms of Help

A commercial loan officer can help design an acceptable business plan, give financial advice, and lend money.

An insurance agent can help you know the risks associated with the business, how to cover risks with insurance, and how to prevent risks with safety devices. Retired executives, volunteers from industry, trade associations, and education who counsel small businesses at low or no cost.

CHAPTER 4:
STRATEGIC AND
BUSINESS PLAN

Planning is bringing the future into the present so that you can do something about it now. Alan Lakein.

Anything that needs to be done deserves to be planned for. That is what will bring success to any human endeavor. Things do not just happen. In this chapter, I want to help you with two types of planning. These plans are strategic and business-oriented. The main difference between the two is the timeline of the plan. I believe that your business is very important to you. For it to be successful, there has to be these plans in place so that they can help give you direction about your business. Some businesses operate without these important plans. But it does not have to be that way because their absence will waste your valuable time. That is, if you act spontaneously without a plan.

A strategic plan is primarily used for implementing and managing the strategic direction of an existing organization. A business plan is used to initially start a business, obtain funding, or direct operations. The two plans cover different timeframes as well. While a strategic plan is a type of business plan, there are several important distinctions between the two types that are worth noting (Brunings, 2017:1). We shall note some of the differences as we deal with each kind of plan.

Strategic plan

And the LORD answered me, and said, Write the vision, and make it plain upon tables, that he may run that readeth it. (Habakkuk 2:3 Webster).

A vision needs to be written down. This also applies to your business. This is because it gives you direction. In order for a vision to be properly pursued, there must be a strategic plan put in place. This will indicate the objectives and action steps with time frames.

What is a strategic plan?

According to Wikipedia, a strategic planning is an organization's process of defining its strategy, or direction, and making decisions on allocating its resources to pursue this strategy. It may also extend to control mechanisms for guiding the implementation of the strategy. So this is about formulating an organization's strategy.

Thompson et al. (2013:6) explain that an organization's strategy consists of the overarching direction set by managers plus the competitive moves and business approaches that they are employing to compete successfully, improve performance, and grow the business. This strategy should answer the following questions:

1) What is our present situation?
2) Where do we want to go from here?
3) How are we going to get there?

According to Thompson et al. (2007:19–20), the managerial process of crafting and executing strategy entails the following:

1) Developing a strategic vision and mission

2) Setting objectives

3) Crafting a strategy to achieve the objectives

4) Implementing and executing the chosen strategy efficiently and effectively

5) Evaluating performance and initiating corrective adjustments

The Purpose of a strategic plan

Brunings (2017:1-2) argues that a strategic plan is primarily used for implementing and managing the strategic direction of an existing organization. Generally, a strategic plan covers a period of three to five years or more. A strategic plan is for established businesses, organizations, and business owners that are serious about growing their organization. This kind of plan is used to provide focus, direction, and action in order to move the organization from where it is now to where it wants to go. A strategic plan is critical to prioritizing resources like time, finances, and people to grow revenue and increase the return on investment.

The plan also focuses on building a sustainable competitive advantage and is futuristic in nature. It is used to communicate the direction of the organization to the staff and stakeholders. Larger organizations with multiple business units and a wide variety of products frequently start their annual planning process with a corporate-driven strategic plan. Departmental plans and marketing plans that work their way down from the strategic plan frequently follow it.

The strategic plan should have the following:

1) Foreword

2) Introduction

3) Background information

4) Vision

5) Mission

6) Values

7) Strategic planning process
8) Environmental analysis
9) Stakeholder analysis
10) Key strategic focus areas or themes
There are different objectives within a focus area.
11) Implementation/Action plan and budget
Each objective has action steps under it. We have columns with subheadings: Activity, responsibility, resource, evaluation measure, and timeline.
12) Monitoring and evaluation
13) Conclusion

Business plan

"For which of you, desiring to build a tower, does not first sit down and count the cost, whether he has enough to complete it? Otherwise, when he has laid a foundation and is not able to finish, all who see it begin to mock him, saying, 'This man began to build and was not able to finish.'" (Luke 14:28–30).

The plans of the diligent lead to profit, as surely as haste leads to poverty. (Proverbs 21:5).

Commit to the Lord whatever you do, and he will establish your plans. (Proverbs 16:3 NIV).

In order to make money in your business, you need to have a plan in place. You need a business plan. It will help you know what needs to be done and when. This plan includes short-term action steps or activities that need to be carried out.

You need the guidance of the Lord on this. He knows better because He is not subject to time. He can see the future now. Where you are limited as a businessperson, He is not. So as you make the plans, invite His guidance.

What is a business plan?

In its simplest form, a business plan is a guide—a roadmap for your business that outlines goals and details how you plan to achieve those goals, according to Berry (2017:1).

The Purpose of a business plan

Explaining what a business plan is, Brunings (2017:1-2) indicates that a business plan is used to initially start a business, obtain funding, or direct operations. It is normally no more than one year. A business plan could be for new businesses or entrepreneurs who are startups. This kind of plan is used to provide a structure for ideas in order to initially define the business. The plan is critical if the business is seeking funding.

The business plan is used to assess the viability of a business opportunity and is more tactical in nature. Furthermore, a business plan is used to present the entrepreneur's ideas to a financial institution. Smaller companies and startup companies typically use only a business plan to develop all aspects of the business on paper, obtain funding, and then start the business. The observation is that many smaller companies, including startups, never develop a strategic plan.

I like the business plan outline given by Varga (1997:12–13). You can use it as a template for developing your own business plan. It is as follows:

1) Type of Business and Product or Service
Here you mention the industry, type of business, and kind of product or service you are dealing with.

2) How it fits you, your talents, skills, experience, and passion
Highlight factors that will enhance the success of your business in terms of your talents, skills, experience, and passion. These are the drivers of success in business. You may not necessarily have all of the above related to the business you are

pursuing. But having some will work to your advantage.

3) What else do you need?

Indicate anything you will need for the success of your business.

4) How your product or service fits today's marketplace

In order to be successful in business, you need to ensure that what you are providing to the market is relevant. The products or services you offer must contribute value to the customers; otherwise, your business might fail even before it starts. People respond to what will satisfy a need.

5) Type of business structure: sole proprietorship, partnership, corporation; officers, Board, employees, contractors, vendors.

The type of business and its leadership structure are described here. The employees, i.e., their positions, should be indicated here. The Board will give strategic direction to your business. The employees will be implementers of the plans to ensure that goals and objectives are met.

All these things are very important to the business, so they have to be clearly indicated.

6) Staying power: available cash, overhead, start-up expenses, income, line of credit

Your business needs to be able to continue operating regardless of circumstances. In business, there are both good and bad times. Some situations are within our control, and some are out of our control. But it has to continue operating. There has to be enough income to pay the organization's obligations and also make a profit because you are in business. Costs should also be manageable. You need to write about it here.

Include cash-flow projections as well as projected income statements and balance sheets.

CHAPTER 5: BUSINESS MANAGEMENT

Effective leadership is putting first things first. Effective management is discipline, carrying it out. Stephen Covey.

"If you are faithful in little things, you will be faithful in large ones. But if you are dishonest in little things, you won't be honest with greater responsibilities." (Luke 16:10 NLT).

"Moreover you shall select from all the people able men, such as fear God, men of truth, hating covetousness; and place such over them to be rulers of thousands, rulers of hundreds, rulers of fifties, and rulers of tens." (Exodus 18:21).

It is scriptural to place able people in positions of leadership. Your business needs to be in the hands of capable men and women in order to achieve its vision and objectives.

What is management?

Management is responsible for coordinating an organization's limited resources in order to achieve specific goals (e.g., the owner buys a new machine that makes coffee faster and saves on labor).

The term "management" designates all activities carried out in the course of running a business venture or organization.

Management may be defined as the planning, organizing, leading, and controlling of human and other resources to achieve all organizational goals efficiently and effectively. Without its four fundamental pillars (the management process), success would be difficult to achieve. The pillars are also called the managerial functions.

What is business management?

It suffices, therefore, to define business management as the planning, organizing, leading, and controlling of a business entity or venture.

The business management functions

Success in management requires learning as fast as the world is changing. [Warren Bennis]

We refer to the major functions of a business as the pillars of any business. Without them, a business entity can fail. They ensure stability and the achievement of the goals and objectives of the business. These pillars include planning, organizing, leading, and controlling.

Planning

Planning is bringing the future into the present so that you can do something about it now. [Alan Lakein]

Planning can be defined as "the thinking that takes place before the action". This is the anticipation of future business environmental trends, predetermining future activities and resource use to meet the challenges and opportunities therein. It includes defining an organization's goals and establishing an overall strategy for achieving those goals. It further puts in place a set of plans or courses of action to integrate and coordinate activities.

So you need to identify appropriate goals (corporate mission and goals) and choose appropriate courses of action (strategy, structure, and function).

The planning process involves:

1) Determining the objectives to be attained in the future
This calls for processes of perception, anticipation, and forecasting future circumstances and requirements.
2) A tool called SWOT (Strengths, Weaknesses, Opportunities, and Threats) analysis helps in assessing the present limitations to the achievement of the set goals and determining how these could be overcome. An entrepreneur needs this in order to weigh the possible options.

Strengths

Strength is something an organization is particularly good at doing or an attribute that enhances its competitiveness in the market. An organization's strengths depend on the quality of its resources and capabilities.
These may include:
1) A powerful strategy supported by good skills and expertise in key areas
2) A strong financial condition; ample financial resources to grow the business
3) A strong brand image or business reputation
4) An attractive customer base
5) A reputation for good customer service
6) Ability to take advantage of economies of scale and/or learning and experience curve effects

Weaknesses

A weakness or competitive deficiency is something an organization lacks or does poorly in comparison to others, or a condition that puts it at a competitive disadvantage in the market. These are weak areas that could be encountered in the project.

Weaknesses can relate to:
1) Inferior or unproven skills, expertise, or intellectual capital in competitively important areas of the business
2) Deficiencies in competitively important physical, organizational, or intangible assets
3) No clear strategic direction
4) A weak balance sheet burdened with too much debt
5) Too narrow a product line relative to rivals
6) Plagued with internal operating problems
7) Behind on product quality

Opportunities

These are environmental functions that can be manipulated to the future advantage of a business.They may include:
1) Serving additional customer groups or expanding into new geographic markets or product segments
2) Expanding the business' product line to meet a broader range of customer needs
3) Transferring the company's skills or technological know-how to new products or businesses
4) Falling trade barriers in attractive foreign markets
5) Openings to take market share away from rival firms

Threats

These are environmental conditions that can cause danger to the business or project in the future.

So basically, planning is about designing actions and programs to progress towards the set goals. Furthermore, it determines future problems likely to occur, the techniques for handling them, and alternative courses of action. This involves the ability to anticipate unforeseen circumstances.

Threats may consist of the following:
1) The likely entry of potent new competitors
2) Loss of sales to substitute products
3) Slowdowns in market growth
4) Costly new regulatory requirements
5) Growing bargaining power of customers and suppliers
6) A shift in buyer needs and tastes away from the industry's product

In summary, planning happens as follows:
1) Setting of goals
This involves the development of the business idea.
2) Formulating a strategy
A strategy gives a guide to future development and expansion. It helps identify any potential bottlenecks in a business process and improves productivity.
3) Implementing the strategy
As you implement the strategy, it will involve planning on a daily basis to ensure production takes place correctly.

The advantages of planning include the following:
1) Facilitates the accomplishment of objectives. The orderliness of planned activities minimizes unnecessary waste of time because everyone involved knows what to do and all other resources are in their proper places.
2) It provides the basis for all other managerial functions (organization and control), as planning defines what is to be done, who should do what, and what resources are required. The organization arranges and relates these resources so as to meet the set objectives.
3) Provides the management with the best possible foresight. It provides the instrument for monitoring and control.
4) Provides the basis for the efficient utilization of resources, avoiding waste of time, material, and human resources.

The following are some of the basic questions often asked during a planning process:

1) What is our problem or need? Who are we? Where are we? What are our norms and values in business?

2) What is our goal?

3) Which way do we all agree to go? Is it feasible? Do we have the resources we need?

4) What are the different ways to reach our goal, and what are the advantages and disadvantages of each way?

5) What tasks must we do to move this way towards our goal?

6) Who will be responsible for the tasks? Who will do what, when, and where?

7) When will we evaluate our progress?

Evaluate the project (self-performance, products). Evaluation needs to be both formative and summative, i.e., before the start of the project and after completion to check on any deviations from set targets. Monitoring should be continuous to be able to correct any deviations in the process. Once all these questions have been discussed in a proposal, the plan can be executed.

Organizing

Organizing involves the assignment of tasks, authority, and resources across the organization. This is a clustering of tasks (job design). It entails the design of systems to ensure effective coordination of resources (human, capital, and natural) across the organizational divide. Establishment of relationships between various clusters of tasks (functions).

Managers are responsible for designing an organization's structure. This determines what tasks need to be done and who will do them. The tasks are grouped; furthermore, the structure indicates who reports to whom and where decisions are to be made. This helps determine the authority relationships (divisions or organizational structures).

Now that you have a plan, you have to make it happen. Is everything ready ahead of your implementation so that the right staff will be channeled to the proper position at the right time? Are your subordinates (families) prepared to do their part of the plan? Is the downstream organization (your customer) ready for what your institution will deliver, and will the outputs be on time? There is more on staffing in Chapter 6.

Leading

Once plans are in place and resources have been organized, the business plan will be ready for implementation. Implementation is not ad hoc. It should have a leader who defines and controls the processes. Since an organization involves people, managers are responsible for directing and coordinating those people.

Management motivates employees, directs the activities of others, and selects the most effective communication channels. At times, there are conflicts among members of an organization, and managers must resolve them.

Leadership is therefore the ability to initiate action, guide others directly, and supervise others in pursuit of a common goal. It comes in different types and can be viewed as:
1) Centralized or decentralized
This depends on the organizational structure and size.
2) Broad or focused
This is dependent on the number of work areas within an organization.
3) Decision-oriented or moral-centered (work or people-focused)
4) Intrinsic or derived from some authority

It is, however, important to clearly distinguish between management and leadership. There is a reciprocal relationship between leadership and management, implying that an effective manager should possess leadership skills while an effective leader should demonstrate management skills. The information box outlines some of the differences between management and leadership.

A leader's mood has some effects on the group that he leads. The leader creates situations and events that lead to positive or negative emotional responses. It should be emphasized that leadership without empathy and effective communication yields no results. Communication is the best motivator for people at the workplace or even at household level.

A manager with good leadership skills should be communicative and be able to motivate family and employees so that they have a sense of belonging or ownership. This leads to a shared vision for the future of the business venture. Where communication is weak and there are no strong motivating points within an organization, the resultant scenario can be a failure.

Controlling

Managers have goals to achieve in an organization. So performance must be monitored. In order to be monitored, performance must be measured. Coordination and control are linked activities that are concerned with monitoring the set tasks and returning them to the correct path if there are any deviations.

Coordination is the act of making different people or things work together for a common goal or effect. Control is the setting of standards, measuring actual performance, and taking corrective action.

Control comprises three main functions:

1) Control of a business consists of seeing that everything is being carried out in accordance with the plan that has been adopted, the orders that have been given, and the principles that have been laid down. Its object is to point out mistakes in order that they may be corrected and prevented from happening again.

2) Control is checking correct performance against pre-determined standards contained in the plans with a view to

ensuring adequate progress and satisfactory performance.
3) Controlling is the measurement and correction of performance in order to make sure that enterprise objectives and the plans devised to attain them are accomplished.

Characteristics of Control include the following:
1) Control is a continuous process.
2) Control is a management process.
3) Control is embedded in each level of the organizational hierarchy.
4) Control is forward-looking.
5) Control is linked with planning.
6) Control is a tool for achieving organizational activities.
Control is effected through information flow, showing the need and importance of communication. Information flow, whether verbal or written, is a form of communication from one party to another.

CHAPTER 6:
RECRUITING PEOPLE

The secret to successful hiring is this: look for the people who want to change the world. - Marc Benioff, CEO of Salesforce.

Whatever you do, work heartily, as for the Lord and not for men, knowing that from the Lord you will receive the inheritance as your reward. You are serving the Lord Christ. – Colossians 3:23-24 (ESV).

So whatever you wish that others would do to you, do also to them, for this is the Law and the Prophets. – Matthew 7:12 (ESV).

Servants, be obedient to them that are [your] masters according to the flesh, with fear and trembling, in singleness of your heart, as unto Christ;

Not with eye service, as men pleasers; but as the servants of Christ, doing the will of God from the heart;

With good will doing service, as to the Lord, and not to men:

Knowing that whatsoever good thing any man doeth, the same shall he receive of the Lord, whether [he be] bond or free.

And, ye masters, do the same things unto them, forbearing threatening: knowing that your Master also is in heaven; neither is there respect of persons with him. (Ephesians 6:5-9 KJV).

"For Scripture says, "Do not muzzle an ox while it is

treading out the grain," and *"The worker deserves his wages."* (1 Timothy 5:18 NIV).

As a business owner, you need skills to operate your business. That means you need to hire and keep talent. This is a big responsibility. Failure to get the right human resources will cause stress and frustration in your business. Achieving business goals may be difficult without the right human skills.

The scriptures above highlight the responsibilities and duties of both the employer and employee. Each party needs to play its part. The golden rule applies to both parties. Each must be able to fit into the shoes of the other for the business to function well.

Recruiting Staff

According to Sher (2000:28), no matter how good your product or service, your entire business depends on people creating, producing, and delivering it to the customer. He further emphasizes the importance of employing the right people because they create a business's culture, its service, its quality, its reputation, and ultimately its profit.

When starting your new business, you may not have the time or the skills to do all the work yourself. You will then need employees for your business. If you employ staff, you will need skills to manage them. You should set objectives for your staff, encourage and motivate them to be productive, supervise them, and pay them correctly. You should also follow the laws and regulations that apply to the labor market.

Staff productivity

Productivity in your business will, to a large extent, depend on the people you employ and the way you manage them. The selection of your staff will therefore greatly influence the results of your business.

The business' productivity and profits will be higher if you recruit the right people for the right job. You will not need full-time employees for every task, but as the tasks will need to be carried out by someone in the business, decide who will be responsible for each task.

Make sure that you, as the owner, can handle all tasks (this is applicable to small businesses). This will help you understand your employees, step in when needed, and eventually reduce your costs.

When you decide to hire staff, it is important to describe exactly what skills and qualifications are required. Unskilled workers may be suitable for some jobs, but other jobs might need staff with special competencies or certain experience.

The first thing to do is to make sure that you know what work is to be done, how much time is to be spent on it, and what skills and experience are required. You make a job description for every position in writing by doing the following:

1) Describe the kind of work (tasks, responsibilities, and position).

2) Estimate the amount of work involved.

3) List the qualifications, skills, and attitudes needed.

Then select the right people by identifying possible candidates or by advertising the job. Some candidates may be promoted heavily by your friends or family. It is important for you to focus on what they are able to do and what they know, not on who they know!

Interview qualified applicants and choose the best person. As soon as you know who to recruit, write a written contract. Ensure that the contract corresponds with the labor law and regulations. Examples of these contracts can be obtained from labor offices, employers' organizations, chambers, or private advisors.

As soon as you have recruited your new workers, prepare and think through an induction program to ensure that a new worker quickly settles in, understands your business, the tasks and responsibilities, and your expectations.

Business and family

Your family and close friends are often an important source of support for the business. Consider the following:

1) Your family and friends are important in providing the moral support needed to start your business.

2) You may obtain guarantees and perhaps some of your start-up capital from members of your family and friends.

3) Family members and friends may easily step in when you run into start-up problems (lack of financial resources and/or personnel).

4) Family members and friends may help you get in contact with important customers and suppliers.

5) Many small businesses involve family members and relatives of close friends as employees. If you want to employ family members or relatives of close friends as staff, you must think about possible problems and make clear "rules."

For example:

1) All personal matters should be kept separate from business.

2) Members of the family and relatives of close friends who are employees should be treated the same as any other staff member.

They should be paid the same wage and have the same opportunities for training and career promotion as other staff. To benefit from your family and relationships, you should remember this advice:

1) Make your family and relatives understand that you want your business to be self-sustaining and that you will not depend on the support of family and friends forever.

2) Make your family and friends understand that the business is yours and that their influence on business decisions should be limited.

3) Keep the money of your business well separated from your private money and from the money of your family.

4) Educate your family members and friends on the basic business principles and explain that the money that comes into the business is to make the business run and to pay for its costs. If you maintain good and constructive relations with your family and friends, you can count on them as good ambassadors for your business. This will help your business achieve improved productivity and higher profits.

CHAPTER 7: BOOKKEEPING AND BUSINESS RECORDS

Making good judgments when one has complete data, facts, and knowledge is not leadership - it's bookkeeping- Dee Hock.

Basic Business concepts

You've had a few ideas about what to produce, and from your research, you now know which products there's a market for. But which of these products will generate the most income? It's worth reminding ourselves of some very basic economic truths before going any further.

The greater the volume of sales and the greater the profit margin for your product, the more income it will generate. Considering the extent to which you can maximize these will help you decide which activity to begin with.

Profit Margin

The profit margin is the difference between the sales price and the cost of that product. Increasing the sales price or lowering product costs will therefore always improve the profit margin.

Sales Price

During your research, you should have gotten a good idea

of the range of prices that might be suitable for your product. For standard agricultural products, prices are often more or less fixed in a fairly tight price range. For less standard products and services, prices can vary considerably.

The sales price directly affects a product's profit margin. It is particularly important, however, because it also affects demand and, therefore, the volume of sales.

Generally, the higher the sales price, the lower the volume of sales, and vice versa. The level at which you set the price will therefore have a dramatic impact on the income generated.

Costs

Lowering costs is a simple way to increase your profit margin. Doing this successfully can, however, be complicated! It is easy to know the sales price of a product, but much harder to know the product's cost accurately. Yet without this, we cannot be sure what the real profit margin is and therefore whether we are really generating income or not.

Income Generated = Volume of Sales x Profit Margin
Profit Margin = Sales Price - Product Cost

Volume of Sales

The volume of sales that can be achieved depends first and foremost on demand, which is heavily influenced by the sales price, as already mentioned. When starting up a new income-generating activity, production capacity will also be an important factor in the volume of sales that can be achieved.

Production Capacity

The resources you are able to dedicate to your income-generating activity will determine your production capacity. Production capacity will be affected by a number of fixed factors.

For example, how much land you have as well as others over which you have more discretion.

It is worth considering at this stage how easy it will be to increase production capacity if your product is successful. Depending on your local environment, hiring extra workers may be easier than acquiring extra land, or vice versa.

Making It Pay

Strategies for maximizing income generation are important. Entrepreneurship is about seeing the opportunities that exist to make money and employing all your skills and resources to exploit them.
A person who wants to generate income has two choices:
1) To produce standard goods better than everyone else.
2) To serve unmet or undermet needs with new products and services.

Within each choice, there will be a number of standard strategies for maximizing income generation that build on the basic economics outlined earlier.

New Products and Unmet or Under-Met Needs

When competition is high, as is often the case with standard products, profit margins are likely to be low. Unless you can be a better producer or provider than your competitors, with higher yields and lower costs, it may be difficult to generate useful income for you from these products.

Under-met Needs

Unless this is the case, demand will be weak and the product will not generate much income, hence the importance of proper market research.

The Value Chain: Capturing and Adding Value

There are a lot of stages involved before a product is sold to the final customer. Someone new will have to turn a profit on their portion of the chain when they take on each stage.

A simple example might be a tomato farmer who sells to a stallholder who sells to the public. The farmer and the stallholder each have to make a profit for it to be worth their while. If the farmer could sell directly to the public without incurring too many additional costs, he might be able to capture more of the value of his product and therefore generate more income this way.

If competition is low, as with new products, profit margins are likely to be much higher. A new product does not have to be entirely new. In fact, it is probably better if it's not, but just one that is not widely available locally. Any successful new product should fulfill an unmet need, or a different example would be if a tomato farmer sold his produce to someone who dried them and then sold them for more money.

The person drying the tomatoes is adding value to them, which is why they can then be sold for more money. If the farmer can add value to his tomatoes by drying them himself without incurring too many additional costs, he can again generate more income in this way.

Depending on the local operating environment, entrepreneurs may find it a useful strategy to try and capture more of the value of their produce, e.g., by selling it through a person-run outlet. An even better strategy, if they are able, would be to add value to their produce, transforming standard products into higher-value ones.

Economies of Scale and the Division of Labor

Normally, the more you can produce of one product, the lower your costs will be. This is known as economies of scale. There are very good reasons for a businessperson to sell many products.

Where, however, a person has a particular advantage in a certain activity, it may generate much more income by focusing on this particular product and producing it on a much larger scale.

Another way to lower production costs is to use the people (employees) you have as efficiently as possible. We noted earlier the obvious link between production capacity and volume of sales, i.e., you can only sell the quantity you're able to produce. More importantly, how much you produce and how you produce it can impact your profit margin.

Bookkeeping and Business Records

When he returned, having received the kingdom, he ordered these servants to whom he had given the money to be called to him so that he might know what they had gained by doing business.(Luke 19:15 ESV).

But what about the servant who does not know what his master wants? He also does things that deserve punishment. But he will get less punishment than the servant who knew what he should do. Whoever has been given much will be responsible for much. Much more will be expected from the one who has been given more." (Luke 12:48).

Accountability is very important for whatever is being done. The owner of the work needs it for various reasons. Accounting for the business transactions carried out in your business is very important. This is done through what we call bookkeeping and record keeping.

Bookkeeping is an important sub-branch of financial accounting, which may be regarded as the foundation on which the entire discipline of accounting is built, according to Dyson (2010:8). This is a system that is used for business record-keeping.

Record-keeping in a business, regardless of its size, is very important. Initially, when one is thinking of starting a business, the need to keep a record of all activities undertaken is not apparent, but once the business has started running, the owner realizes the need for bookkeeping and accounting.

Record-keeping should begin from the first minute one spends any amount of money on any business idea. Recording all transactions will help the businessperson keep abreast of establishment costs initially, running expenses, and business revenue once the business starts bringing in cash.

If you are like most entrepreneurs, you feel passionately about your business idea. You are convinced you will succeed. Setting up a record-keeping system may not be at the top of your list of things to do as you put together a plan and struggle to find the capital to start your business. But keeping good records may be the key to success.

Unless you maintain an accurate account of sales, expenses, and cash flow, the best idea in the world will not yield concrete results. Your accounting system provides the information you need to make solid, informed decisions about the operation of your business. It also provides the basis for income-tax and sales-tax reporting.

If you plan to hire employees, your business must maintain records meeting the requirements of the state and local agencies that levy taxes and regulate employer-employee relations.

If you expect to have more than one or two employees, consider hiring a payroll service to maintain these records and see that your payroll taxes are paid on time. You don't have to be a certified public accountant to operate a small business, but you should have a rudimentary understanding of accounting before you open the doors.

Bookkeeping can be a very simple exercise where one records in an exercise book all the activities that are undertaken for business purposes. The owner of the business should record such

important issues as:
1) Amounts paid for licenses and permits initially
2) Costs incurred to secure the location
3) Costs spent on travel for purposes of the business
4) The amount used to buy the initial stock and how much was actually bought
5) Daily sales, cash, and credit
6) Daily expenses and withdrawals
7) Daily purchases
8) Daily cash balances

Simple bookkeeping and accounting assist the businessperson in determining whether a profit or loss is the end result of the business. The records will also help in actually pinpointing which activities are taking up more cash than they should and which activities are bringing in more money. The businessperson can set a saving target and a collection target for customers taking goods on credit.

When recording credit transactions, it is important to record dates, type and amount of goods, amount paid as a deposit, and the amount pending. It has been known that credit transactions cause conflict between people if they are not recorded properly.

Cash transactions should also be recorded properly so that the type, cost, and price of goods sold can be determined. Cash balances should be determined at the end of every day so that the balances at the beginning of the day and the balances at the end of the day can be determined. It is prudent to keep complete records of business transactions and to consult someone who understands accounting to set up an easy method of keeping records that is useful and also tracks the performance of the business.

Accounting is the language of business; without accounting, business will be dumb. A trader or a person engaged in business at any level, from the milk sellers on the roadside to the owners of the big wholesaling businesses, cannot escape the idea of accounting and record-keeping. Accounting is just a tool for recording, storing, and analyzing business activities in terms of money.

Accounting operates on the idea that all business activities are of two kinds: one that receives and the other that gives.
Examples:
1) If you sell an item for cash, you give away the item and get the cash. Your cash increases while your stock decreases.
2) When you pay salary, your cash decreases, and salary payments to your employees increase. In accounting, the world is also divided into just two things: what you own, called your assets, and what you owe to other people, called your liabilities.
Using these two straightforward concepts, accounting entails recording business transactions in books of accounts, which can be as straightforward as entries in a blank exercise book or as sophisticated as computer-based accounting systems.

It is important that a businessperson keep an updated cash book and a ledger.

1) Cash Book

The cash book records all activities related to the cash transactions. It records how much cash has come in and how much has gone out. All cash receipts and payments are traced in this book.

2) Ledger

The ledger records all items and also records dates and amounts under them. For example, a salary entry in the ledger will have the amount paid, the period for which it was paid, the day and date it was paid, and to whom it was paid.

People typically keep in mind and rely on a lot of the

activities that businesses undertake. Oral agreements are entered into without evidence of the agreements. Trust is good, but keeping and witnessing records is better. Anything can happen to an individual, and memory is fickle. Records tell the truth. They prevent fraud and other malpractices and protect business assets.

Since accounting and record-keeping are not profit-making activities, they should be kept simple, easy to understand, and affordable. If well managed, accounting records help in making decisions and also offer security for the business's assets.

At the end of the period, revenues are totaled and expenses are subtracted to arrive at a profit or loss. Also, a statement is made of the assets the business owns and the debts it owes to calculate the profit of the business.

Example of a ledger account taken from Dyson (2010:56) with a slight modification:

Joe Simple: Sole Trader

The following information relates to Joe Simple, who started a new business on July 1, 2014:
(1) 1/07/14   Joe started the business with E5, 000 in cash.
(2) 3/07/14   He paid E3,000 of the cash into a business bank account.
(3) 5/07/14   Joe bought a van for E2 000 paying by check.
(4) 7/07/14   He bought some goods, paying E1,000 in cash.
(5) 9/07/14   Joe sold some of the goods, receiving E1 500 in cash.
Required:
Enter the above transactions in Joe's ledger accounts.
Answer:
Joe Simple's books of account:

Cash Account					
		E			E
01/07/2014	Capital (1)	5000	03/07/2014	Bank (5)	3000
09/07/2014	Sales (5)	1500	07/07/2014	Purchases (4)	1000

Capital Account					
		E			E
01/07/2014	Capital (1)	5000			

Bank Account					
		E			E
03/07/2014	Cash (2)	3000	05/07/2014	Van (3)	2000

Van Account					
		E			E
05/07/2014	Bank (3)	2000			

Purchases Account					
		E			E
05/07/2014	Cash (4)	1000			

Sales Account					
		E			E
			09/07/2014	Cash (5)	1500

Notes:

The numbers in brackets after each entry refer to the example notes; they have been inserted for guidance only.

The narration relates to that account in which equal and opposite entries may be found.

After entering all the transactions for a particular period in appropriate ledger accounts, the next stage in the exercise is to calculate the balance on each account at the end of an accounting period.

You then compile what is called a trial balance. According to Dyson (2010:59), a trial balance is a working paper compiled at the end of a specific accounting period. This is not part of the double-entry procedure.

It has three main purposes, which are:

1. To check that all of the transactions for a particular period have been entered correctly in the ledger system.
2. To confirm that the balance on each account is correct.
3. To assist in the preparation of the profit and loss (Income and Expenditure) account and the balance sheet.

3) Income and expenditure account (Income statement)

A statement of income and expenses is known as an income statement, and a statement of assets and liabilities is called a balance sheet. The information from these statements helps the business owner know whether the business is profitable or not. The information also assists the businessperson in reaching a decision about the business, whether to expand, close, or continue with the current operations as they are. A statement to show all the cash received from the business and the way it has been spent can also help in showing the sources and uses of the cash in the business.

A business without records and proper financial accounting is bound to face challenges. Effective business planning and control encompass good record-keeping (material and financial) and effective financial accounting.

Record Keeping

Business planning depends on analyzing past performance, identifying the strengths and weaknesses of the business, and using this knowledge to make both present and future decisions. The basis for such analysis is sound, accurate information, which can only be obtained from good records. Although a great number of records can be kept, the businessperson must decide what information he or she requires for his or her planning. Records that are never used are a waste of time and resources.

Financial management

Financial management is about planning income and expenditure and making decisions that will enable you to survive financially (CISP, 2014:35).

Financial planning is about:

1) Making sure that the business can survive
Lack of cash flow can bring your business to its knees. Why? Your products will need cash to be available for trade. The people who are working will need to be paid, as will creditors.

2) Ensuring that money is being spent in the most efficient way
Cash must be directed mostly toward things that bring in money. Otherwise, your business can suffer due to unproductive spending.
3) Making sure that the money is being spent to fulfill the objectives of the business
Here we can see that planning is very important. The objectives of the business are set during planning, and they are a guide to the operations of the business. So carrying out the activities that are in the plan will ensure the right course.
4) Being able to plan for the future of the business in a realistic

way

The financial accounts of a business, including the profit and loss accounts and the balance sheet, can be calculated from the financial records, such as the wage book, cash book, invoices, etc.

What you need

You have to record all the money coming into your business and all the money going out. This is to keep track of the cash flow.

To do this, you will need:

1) To record every sale.

Cash Sales in receipts
Non-cash sales in invoices

2) To receive invoices or issue receipts for every purchase or make a simple journal entry.

Purchases Paid
Purchases Unpaid

3) Keep a record of all payments in and out of your cash.
4) If you cannot afford a computerized accounting program, keep a simple cashbook for recording such information. It records all cash coming into and going out of the business.

Simple rules for small business bookkeeping

1) Record every sale as cash or credit.
2) Separate records of sales into cash or credit
3) Keep the sales to every credit customer separate.
4) When a customer pays, keep a proper record of that payment or issue a receipt and update the customer's balance.
5) Record your non-sales income, such as grants and asset disposals, in your cash book.
6) Record every purchase as cash or credit.
7) Separate records of purchases into cash or credit

8) Keep purchases from every supplier separate.

9) When you pay a supplier, deduct the amount from the cash book and update the supplier's balance.

10) At the end of the month, update all your records.

11) Calculate your total sales, purchases, expenses, and cash.

12) To arrive at the profit,

Profit is calculated as total sales minus total purchases minus expenses.

Drawings from the business

When running a business, the owner may have to withdraw some money from the business once in a while. The capital invested in the business is seed money and needs to be protected until it grows and matures. When the business is growing, it is important to reinvest the profits in the business. The expenses of the owner should be limited enough to make life comfortable, and no luxury expense may be withdrawn from the business while it is still in its infancy.

The purpose of doing business is to improve one's life, to care for one's family, and to contribute to society. The success of the business is vital for all these objectives to be achieved. Removing money from the business reduces the funds available to the business for investments and affects its cash flows.

When withdrawing funds from the business, it is important to look at the business's performance. You can only withdraw if the business is doing well enough to make a sufficient profit. You also have to consider the timing of the withdrawal. There must be sufficient cash to pay debts and other obligations before you can withdraw for personal reasons.

The business owner may need to withdraw money for personal survival purposes. These will be treated as a salary as an employee of the business. These drawings will help the owner meet the food, shelter, clothing, and education needs of his or her family. The business can only make a profit if it can pay those who work for it, including the owner, sufficient wages to survive. The owner may not get paid at market rate but should at least be paid enough to be able to pay for important expenses.

When the business is successful and money is available, the owner should have the liberty to spend money rightly and contribute generously to society without jeopardizing the business operations.

CHAPTER 8: MARKETING YOUR BUSINESS

Clients don't care about the labor pains; they want to see the baby- Tim Williams.

Starbucks is not an advertiser; people think we are a great marketing company, but in fact we spend very little money on marketing and more money on training our people than advertising- Howard Schultz.

You can't sell anything if you can't tell anything- Beth Comstock.

For you to make money from your business, you must be able to sell goods or provide services. Goods and services are bought by customers. Customers do not just dream about what you are selling; they need to be informed about it by someone. Failure to market is like sitting in a dark place; you know you are there, and you hope people will find you.

Customers have to get those goods to a place they can access. For example, if you start the business of making beautiful dresses for ladies, all the ladies within the area must know about it before they buy. Customers do not appear out of nowhere. They must hear of your business before they will ever call you, and that is the purpose of marketing.

What is marketing? Essentially, it is anything you do to promote your business, get your name remembered, and generate sales. It encompasses promotions, giveaways, publicity, customer relations, public speaking, signs, and anything else that keeps your business in the public eye and brings customers in the door.

Marketing, according to Kotler et al. (2016:27), is about identifying and meeting human and social needs. A formal definition by The American Marketing Association, cited in Kotler et al. (2016:27), is offered as the activity, set of institutions, and processes for creating, communicating, delivering, and exchanging offerings that have value for customers, clients, partners, and society at large. They further indicate that what can be marketed includes goods, services, events, experiences, persons, places, properties, organizations, information, and ideas.

Sher (2000:26) defines marketing as the machine that drives your business. He further asserts that good marketing brings people who are happy to part with their money in exchange for your products or services to your door.

Marketing tries to understand customer needs, assists in the production process, and then assists in moving the goods or services from producer to consumer. That results in customer satisfaction. But satisfaction is more than just customer satisfaction. It includes a range of stakeholders, all of whom are affected by the marketing activities.

Make a list, or just name ten sources of business or ten ways you can attract customers. If you are going to make your business a success, you will need to be creative and come up with many different ways to generate sales.

Methods that you can use to promote your business

Signs

A big, bold sign in the right location can be a very effective way to bring in new business. Retail businesses swear by good signage. A number of different factors need to be considered when choosing a sign:

1) From what distance do you want the sign to be seen?
You should not put up a sign just for the sake of it. Ensure that people can see it. Even someone who is in a car should be able to see it.
2) Do you want it to be seen at night?
3) What kind of weather will it be exposed to?
The sign should withstand any weather condition. Otherwise, it might be spoiled, and thus your money will be lost.
4) How much can you afford to spend?
Look around for different quotations. At the end of it all, the quality of the material used will be important. It will determine the durability of your sign.
5) Can you legally put up the sign you desire?
Check the local requirements in your area. If your proposed sign is illegal, you will first need to get clearance from the authority.

Testimonials

Customer satisfaction is very important for your business. Satisfied customers can be your best sales tools, as they lend credibility to your business. Testimonials are powerful because these people have experience; they have handled and tasted your product or service. So they talk about something they really know.

Excellence

It has been said that it costs five times more to create a new client than to retain an existing one. A satisfied customer will spread the good word about your business to at least one other person, while an unhappy customer will likely complain to many more than that. See how much poor service can cost your business? Doing great work and offering superior customer service can go a long way toward creating continuing revenue.

Networking

You cannot succeed alone. So networking is very important, and it begins with your friends and family. Make sure that they know how much you value new business and appreciate referrals. Networking is particularly critical for local service businesses. For certain types of specialized professional consulting fields, such as salons and beauty shops or tailors, networking can make a huge difference.

Advertising on Radio

Advertising on radio is a simple way to let a lot of people know about your product. Therefore, make use of it.

Internet marketing

With the introduction of the internet, different platforms can be used to expose your business. You can blog, write articles, and use social media. These are very useful platforms for promoting your business.

Where is the market for your product?

The following steps can be used to check whether there is likely to be a market for your product:

1) Observe the various activities within your community.
Where do the people come together or congregate? You can use places like hospitals, schools, public offices, religious institutions, industries, and local produce markets. What do people need in those areas? For example, non-prescription medicine, school uniforms, refreshments, food, etc.

2) What are the needs of the people in your community?
You can ask the people in your community what products or services they are interested in.

3) Find out what activities are allowed in those areas.
Finding out what is and is not allowed in business can save you a great deal of time. Also, find out where and when not to do business.

4) Collect information about similar businesses.
It is best to know similar businesses in your locality. Get to know where they sell their products, whether at home, an open-air market, shops, stalls, or vending, depending on what your business is. Check the prices that your rivals are charging. They may be selling substitutes for your products. If customers feel your product is more expensive when compared with substitute products, they will go for them.

Further, collect information on the following questions:

1) Do they sell all the time, or do they sell on a seasonal basis?
2) What equipment do they use?
3) How many businesses failed, and why did they fail?
5) Find out about the buyers of your product.

Estimate the number of people who will buy from you. You should know your customers, i.e., their age group, income, and other factors. Ask yourself why they will buy from you and not the next person. Also, find out where they usually buy.
6) Find out about the source of your product; where will you get it from?
Know where you will source your stock. Try to ensure that it is not in one place. If it is from one place, the supplier will have more bargaining power over you. That may not be favorable. You must be able to change stock suppliers if the existing ones are not good.

The location of the supplier of your product is very important for cost control. The issue of transport needs to be sorted. Readily available transport will improve efficiency in providing good service to your customers. Consider whether or not you will use your own transport or the supplier's.

Know the prices of your suppliers as well as their terms of payment.

7) What are some of the things that can harm your business?

Culture

There are different definitions of culture. Maitah (2017:4-5) gives a number of these definitions. However, I picked up the following ones:

1) Culture is the collective programming of the mind that distinguishes the members of one human group from another.

2) Culture is the guide for the selection of appropriate responses in social situations, social interactions, and business interactions.

3) A system of values and norms that are shared among a group of people and that, when taken together, constitute a design for living

When it comes to business, ensure that you understand the culture of the people who form your market because culture affects consumer behavior, local demand, buying decisions, and brand image. Furthermore, culture defines a set of acceptable and unacceptable behaviors that form the basis of a "way of doing business". That will help you provide what they value. If you provide what is against their culture, you will miss the market and fail in business, and I know you do not want that.

Competition

According to Business Case Studies, the presence of competitors helps to drive down the profit that a firm can make. Competition in business occurs when many firms sell identical products and act independently to supply their products to the same group of consumers. (IAC Publishing, 2017:1).

Other factors that can harm your business are as follows:
1) Insecurity
2) Suppliers
3) Climate
4) Local regulations
5) Weather and Climate
6) Environment

What are the skills needed to run this business?

It is important to have the knowledge and skills to run the type of business you own. If you do not have them yourself, hire someone who does or outsource them. However, that should be profitable for you since this is a business. Have knowledge of the product you want to sell. Ignorance may lead to many problems. Customers must receive help if they have problems with your product. Know where you will sell your product or service. It may be at home, an open-air market, stalls, a shop, on the Internet, etc.

Marketing on a Budget

Marketing is a strategy to get your name known by the public so that when they need a product or service, they think of your business. The great thing about marketing is that there are plenty of cheap ways to get business without spending a lot of money. The following cost-effective ideas can definitely increase sales, and they need not cost a fortune. The key is to choose the methods that are appropriate for your business, marketplace, and style.

1) Gifts and Samples

A gift allows present customers to introduce you to new customers. Even better, since you get paid up front, it helps your cash flow.

A free gift reminds your customer of you and your service.

Just about anything can be engraved, imprinted, silk-screened, or embroidered with your company name and phone number. This may be done on pens, key chains, coffee mugs, refrigerator magnets, caps, paperweights, etc. Giving potential customers a free sample is an excellent way to attract attention and make a positive impression. However, if your product is too expensive to give away outright, you can offer a free trial to qualified customers.

2) Brochures

A good brochure is a great selling tool that allows you to provide plenty of information about your business quickly and inexpensively. This helps a customer have enough information to make a decision to buy.

3) Packaging

The plastic bags that customers leave your store with can be great, cost-effective signs. With your name, address, phone number, and logo on the side, bags can be a valuable marketing tool.

4) Speeches

Depending on your topic and your market, you might want to speak before business meetings, parent groups, senior citizens, or other local organizations. This can help you boost the sales of your product without incurring extra costs.

5) Word-of-mouth advertising

The best source of repeat business is happy customers. Make sure that your current customers know how valuable they are to you. Give something for free to loyal customers as a way to say thank you. This is very effective as potential customers receive testimonies about your product or service.

6) Donations

Donating your product or service to a charitable cause often results in positive exposure. Some companies invite the presence of the media, and such gestures become part of the news. Many people want to help by purchasing products from a company that donates to charitable causes.

7) Press releases

A well-written press release sent to the right media outlet can generate a free story about you and your business that can be used for sales, reproduced, and used again and again to create credibility.

8) Trade shows

Specialized trade shows allow business owners to promote, sell, network, and check out the competition in one location. Trade shows are great for the small business entrepreneur because they pack a lot of potential into a short time and need not cost a lot. In order to be successful at a trade show, you need a booth that attracts attention because there are so many booths. That means you need to be creative and put some time into planning your booth before the show.

Advertising

It takes a big idea to attract the attention of consumers and get them to buy your product. Unless your advertising contains a big idea, it will pass like a ship in the night. I doubt if more than one campaign in a hundred contains a big idea, says David Ogilvy.

Not advertising is like being alone in a dark room—you know you are there, but no one else is. The whole idea of almost all advertising is to turn on the light and let people know you are there. You have to get people to come into the store. Advertising will do that. If you have very high-quality goods or can provide excellent services and you are the only one who knows that you have these products, then it will do you no good. If you run a private school that is integrated, has excellent classes, good teachers, and a library, but parents in the town do not know that, then it will be of no use. Advertising is a method of making your customers aware of what you have, where you are, and what kind of service they can expect from you. Sometimes it is a way of attracting customers to new businesses; other times it is a way of reminding them of an existing business or product.

Advertising Alternatives

1) Newspapers

Advertising in the newspaper is a great, inexpensive way to reach a large audience. Newspaper ads can be used to promote a sale, grab attention, or offer specials on your product or service. The downside is that newspapers carry lots of ads, so yours can get lost.

2) Magazines

Magazine ads cost more than those in the paper, but magazines stay in the house longer than a newspaper, so the price may be worth it. Magazines are especially good for promoting your image and building your brand. Trade magazines are useful for business-to-business advertising. Magazines come out periodically and are usually targeted at a specific audience.

3) Radio

Radio can be an inexpensive, high-impact way to reach a specific market. Repetition is essential with radio advertising, as studies show that it often takes someone hearing your ad six times before it sinks in. One needs to understand a radio station's differences, their target audience, and their coverage before placing an ad. Radio advertising works and helps inform potential clients about your products and services.

Radio can be a very cost-effective way to advertise your business; it is fairly easy to target your market by advertising on the appropriate show. As there are two stations in most areas catering to dozens of different tastes, your job is to find the station and the show that best attract your desired demographic. Once you do that, call the station and make an appointment with a sales representative. He or she will be glad to help you write an ad and will even produce it for you for little or no cost. The trick with radio advertising is to be clever and grab the listener's attention. Humor, music, and sound effects can all be used to great effect on the radio.

Notice which ads grab your attention, and model your own ad after that. There is no need to reinvent the wheel. The important thing to remember with radio ads is that repetition is the key. Repetition is the key. Repetition is the key. Say it enough, and your audience will remember your ad.

4) Television

Television advertising is very effective but correspondingly expensive. Television advertising works, but there are no clear television stations targeting this region, and it may not be cost-effective for a small businessperson to place an ad on any of the main television stations.

5) Internet

With the internet, the means of advertising have increased. Internet advertising is not expensive. You can choose platforms that work for you. It may be article writing, email marketing, blogging, social network advertising, etc.

6) Outdoor or billboards

Outdoor advertising or billboards offer high visibility, and the cost per viewer is relatively low. Billboards are like signs and are visible to many people.

How to make a good advertisement

If you choose to advertise, you must create an ad that attracts customers. Interestingly, all ads, no matter the medium, are fairly similar in structure. They all must grab attention and make an offer. One simple way to create a successful ad for radio is to follow the following steps:

1) Attention

The first thing you have to do is grab their attention. Once you do that, you can get a potential customer interested in what you are selling. If you don't get their attention, they will not receive your message among the distractions of the headline news, sports stories, and other more distinctive ads. You must first hit your prospect between the eyes with a powerful headline. A good headline will grab a customer by the throat, show them the benefit of hearing more, and do so in two or three seconds. When writing your ad, keep in mind that the benefits that are most likely to get attention include saving money, saving time, making money, and better health.

2) Interest and Desire

After you have the prospect's attention, you have to make your pitch in the body of the ad. You do that by making the customer a compelling offer and describing as many benefits as possible in simple and interesting terms. Because the product or service must fill a market need to be successful, you must explain how it does that. Your ad must be well written so it clearly explains the benefits to customers and keeps their attention.

3) Action

Finally, you must ask for the order. Give reasons for the customer to buy now, and make it easy for him or her to do so. This will involve a coupon for mail orders, a toll-free order line, an e-mail address, an online order form, a fax order line, or any other means to make it easy and simple to order. Be sure to take the fear out of the purchase as much as possible by giving guarantees, offering testimonials, and showing how the customer is going to miss out if he doesn't order NOW!

Essential information in any advertisement:

1) What is the business?
2) What are the products and services on sale?
3) The place of the business
4) Why should the buyers visit the business?
5) If there are special prices or sales
6) Contact phone number
7) When the business is open

Possible distribution channels
1. Direct to Consumers

Advantages
1) By so doing, you can maintain the full retail price without paying margins to wholesalers and retailers.
2) Self-retailing aids active promotion.
3) Some types of products may not require packaging.
4) Transport problems may be limited.
5) Direct communication from customers receiving constructive criticism

Disadvantages
1) Time-consuming (compromises on processing and focuses on product movement)
2) Business expansion may be limited as distribution is limited to a few locations.

3) Transport logistics may be costly, especially where little product is concerned.

4) Compromise on pricing if produce is not continuously bought.

2. Selling to Retailers

Advantages

1) Large volumes can be moved as more outlets can be reached.

2) Increased devotion to processing, thus improving quality

Disadvantages

1) Compromise on the selling price, as some proceeds go to the retailer.

2) Products that need to be transported and stocks replenished when they run out may be likely to be bought at a fixed price rather than negotiated.

3. Selling to wholesalers

Advantage

Since a lot of retailers visit wholesalers, they can expose your products to much more customers and sell them over a larger geographic area than you could on your own.

Disadvantages

1) Wholesalers' minimum quantity requirements are huge and may be difficult for small-scale producers to fulfill.

2) The prices offered are too low because they need to take a margin to make a profit.

4. Selling to government institutions, International organizations, and the hospitality industry:

Advantages

1) Can be supplied under fixed agreements, including quantity.

2) There is no need to worry about promotion.

Disadvantage

Government institutions are normally too slow to settle their bills.

5. Selling to visiting traders

Advantages
1) There are no worries about transport and packaging as they purchase from the farm gate.
2) Minimizes the trader's workload in terms of time spent selling produce.

Disadvantages
1) Traders may have insufficient funds
2) Too many negotiations resulting in lower prices

Principles of Marketing

Marketing is the management process that identifies, anticipates, and satisfies customer requirements profitably. This satisfaction is achieved through the provision of the products the market requires:

1) Setting prices that the market is willing to pay
2) Getting products and/or services to the market
3) Making information available and attracting the market to buy your products and services

Marketing is an important part of starting and running a business. It does not matter how good your product or service is; if you do not market it in the right way, no one will buy it. Marketing never stops; all the time you are running your business, you should listen to your customers' wishes, sell good products, or provide good services.

Your marketing starts with your business idea. Using your business idea as the starting point, you need to learn more about your customers and competitors through market research to make your marketing plan.

In essence, marketing is a four-step process that begins with:
1) Analyzing and defining a qualified universe of potential users and buyers
2) Capturing the attention of the intended buyers within the targeted zone
3) Systematic effort is being put into getting the prospects to accept the concepts or propositions offered via the marketing effort.
4) Conversion of the prospective buyer into an actual buyer by getting them to take the desired action

When you decide to get into serious business, for success to be registered, have a clear intention. Know what you want to be, do, and have. Furthermore, take consistent action. Do the things necessary to achieve the desired outcome.

Market Research

Market research is the carrying out of a feasibility study to determine market trends in a given area or population. It is the process of investigating a market in order to find out the sales prospects for a product and how to achieve success. It is more than the analysis of raw data. It is an opportunity to look outside your company for factors that may affect your success.

Market research is essential before beginning any venture because there is a risk that consumers do not need or want the product or do not like its packaging or presentation. There is also the possibility that the price the processor wants to charge is too high for the customers to afford. Hence, market research is essential to ensure that agro-processing can be carried out efficiently, effectively, and profitably.

There are several ways of carrying out market research:
1) Talking to potential customers, asking them what products or services they want to buy and what they think about your

competitors
2) Study your competitors' businesses. Find out about their products or services, e.g., Quality design, pricing, and how they attract customers.
3) Ask suppliers and business friends which goods sell well in their businesses, what they think about their businesses, and what they think about your competitors' products.
4) Read newspapers, catalogs, trade journals, and magazines to get information and ideas on new products or services.
5) Having done thorough research on the market, the marketing plan would then need to be put in place.

The marketing plan

A marketing plan is the map that, when complete, will reveal a clear route to your prospective customers. A good marketing plan must reveal specific items of information.

A marketing plan should help you accomplish the following:
1) Prove that you understand your industry. Knowing your product is not enough.
2) Identify your market. These are the people most likely to buy your product or use your services.
3) Identify your competitors. Who's out there, and what are they doing?
4) Establish your pricing, distribution, and product positioning. How much will it cost, plus a fair profit? How will you get there? And where do you fit into the market?
5) Get someone to subsidize your dream. If you want to attract customers, a written marketing plan is essential.
6) Focus on a single, effective marketing concept. Define your best strength and lead with that.

A successful marketing plan is based on research and analysis. But because information can be manipulated to prove almost anything, insight is equally important. Once market research has been done and a marketing plan drawn, the marketing mix should come into play, where there is interplay between the product, pricing, positioning, and promotion to effect organizational profits.

According to Varga (1997:14–15), your marketing plan should contain the following:
1) Initial product/service description
2) Product/service line
3) Approach to customer: wholesale, distributor, franchise, chains, retail, direct
4) Unique position in the marketplace
5) Competition
6) Costs, sale price, and profits
7) Approach to the marketplace: PR, advertising, brochures, direct mail, letters
So once you have the above sections filled out, you have your marketing plan. You are ready to work and promote your business.

The Marketing Mix

The marketing mix is traditionally a complement of the 4 Ps, but recently three more Ps were coined; hence, it is now known as the 7 Ps.

These elements include:

Product: it should be of high quality and well presented. The attributes to consider are branding, packaging, and appearance as they relate to customer needs and wants.
Price: refers to the process of setting the price for the product, including discounts. The commodity price should be commensurate with production costs and quality. There is also a need to understand the competitors' pricing policies and demand-driven pricing.
Placement (distribution): This refers to how the product gets to the customer. This also refers to how the environment in which the product is sold can affect sales.

When deciding where to sell the product, one has to consider:
1) The perishability of the commodity
2) The consumer of the product
3) The competing products
4) Transport availability and cost
5) The quantities that can go through that particular market

Promotion: This is making people aware of what you have on offer and enticing them to buy. This involves public relations, sales promotions, and advertising.

People: self-presentation for market appreciation Any person coming into contact with customers can have an impact on their overall satisfaction. Whether as part of a supporting service to a product or involved in a total service, people are particularly important because, in the customer's eyes, they are generally inseparable from the total service. "Proof is often no more vice." These people should be appropriately trained, well-motivated, and the right people.

Process: this is the process involved in providing a service and the behavior of people, which can be crucial to customer satisfaction. When production and marketing start, there should be continuity and uniformity of purpose.

Physical evidence: Unlike a product, a service cannot be experienced before it is delivered, which makes it intangible. This, therefore, means that potential customers could perceive greater risk when deciding whether to use a service. To reduce the feeling of risk and thus improve the chance for success, it is often vital to offer potential customers the chance to see what a service would be like. This is done by providing physical evidence, such as case studies, testimonials, or demonstrations.

Once the marketing plan has been drawn up and the marketing mix modeled, the entrepreneur should be ready to introduce the product to the market. However, marketing mix modeling is not a once-off event but a continuous process throughout the life of the enterprise. Once the market has been penetrated, the entrepreneur should position the product as one of the best.

Market Positioning

Market positioning is the ability to create an image within the market. An image is the outward representation of being who you want to be, doing what you want to do, and having what you want to have. Positioning yourself can lead to personal fulfillment. Being in someone else's position limits your opportunities and choices. Your position in the market evolves by defining the characteristics of your product. If you don't define your product, the competition will do it for you.

The primary elements of positioning are:
Pricing: Is your product a luxury item, somewhere in the middle, or cheap?
Quality: total quality is a much-used and abused phrase. But is your product well-produced? What controls are in place to assure consistency? Do you back your quality claim with customer-friendly guarantees?
Service: do you offer the added value of customer service and decisions?

Market positioning can also give way to market segmentation, which involves breaking up the market into identical subsets. These subsets are divided according to their needs for purposes of marketing intensity.

This makes it easy to:

1) Target profitable areas.
2) Satisfy customers
3) Create a territory for one's products.
4) Introduce new products.

However, the challenges faced by small-scale traders are

manifold, most of them man-made. Traders usually lack business management skills:

1) Lack of marketing skills
2) Do not do any market research.
3) Depend on ad hoc marketing
4) Approach the market at the end of the production cycle.

There is therefore a need to change this behavior and inculcate a sense of entrepreneurship so that they realize the potential they have. Having noted that farmers are not keen on conducting market research, they can get information from market information services.

Research the Market

By now, you may already have a few ideas about which kinds of activities and products will offer the best opportunities for generating income. You've already considered the local market; now's the time to test your assumptions and actually research it. Lack of sufficient market research is a major factor in why so many new enterprises fail. Don't just assume; do some research!

Assessing Demand

How you assess demand, how easy it is, and how accurate it is will depend on whether the product is more or less identical to an existing product already sold, e.g., laptops, milk, meat, etc. For such products, the greater the demand, the greater the opportunity for sales—if you can produce them at the right price, of course! Where products are new to your market or differ substantially based on their quality, they will be harder to assess.

Observation

For products similar to ones already on sale, simple observation can be enough to provide a good idea of demand.

1) How much of the product is sold in an hour?
2) At what price?
3) What types of customers are buying it?

The more outlets you can look at, the better your understanding will be of the factors that shape demand.
1) How does the price of the product affect sales?
2) How much does the price vary between different outlets?
3) How does the type of outlet affect sales?
4) How does the location of the outlet affect sales?
5) How does the presentation of the outlet or product affect sales?

Market Surveys

For new markets or new products, surveys can be a good way of assessing likely demand. Surveys can take the form of a questionnaire conducted in person or by mail.

The larger the number of people surveyed, the better your results will be. The more focused the questions and the more limited the choice of answers you offer participants, the easier it will be to draw conclusions from the results.

Asking as wide a cross-section of the population as possible —i.e., old, young, men, women, rich, poor, etc.—to take part in your survey is very useful. If you asked only young people or only older people, for instance, it is likely that you would get different results.

By including a diverse mix of people, you will get a good idea not only of demand but also of who your best target market might be. This can then help you select a suitable group of people to take part in a focus group.

Focus Groups

A complementary approach to surveys, which is being used

more and more, is that of focus groups. Here, you take a small group of people from your target market and get them talking in a very open way about themselves and your product. By listening carefully to what they like and dislike about your product and how it fits into their lives, you will get very useful information on the factors that shape demand.

The information from surveys and focus groups will not only give you a good picture of demand, but it can also be used to help you improve your product and decide how to best promote it.

The Holistic marketing concept

Regent Business School (2007:19) describes holistic marketing as the development, design, and implementation of marketing programs, processes, and activities that recognize the breadth and interdependencies of their effects. In essence, everything matters. Its broad view includes four (4) areas that were traditionally seen as quite separate, which are described as follows:

1) Relationship marketing

A customer-centered approach that recognizes that the customer is at the center of a chain, or network, of relationships between various stakeholders. Salespeople working with key customers must do more than call only when they think customers might be ready to place orders. Instead, they should call or visit at other times and make useful suggestions about the business. It is advised that they monitor key accounts and know the problems of the customers.

2) Internal marketing

The view is that marketing should be part of a company philosophy that includes all staff in an effort to bring customer satisfaction to their clients. Internal marketing requires everyone in the organization to accept the concepts and goals of marketing and engage in choosing, providing, and communicating customer value.

Once all the employees realize that their duty is to create, serve, and satisfy customers, the company becomes an effective marketer.

3) Integrated marketing

The view that the four Ps (product, place, price, and promotion) should be brought together in a marketing mix to satisfy customers. Integrated marketing is about mixing and matching marketing activities to maximize their individual and collective effects. Marketers need a variety of activities that will enforce the brand promise to achieve this.

4) Social responsibility marketing

This is about the incorporation of cause marketing, cause-related marketing, corporate philanthropy, corporate community involvement, and socially responsible business practices.

Marketers must consider the legal, environmental, ethical, and social context of their role and activities since the effects of marketing do not end with the company. Instead, they extend to the customer and to society as a whole.

Making contributions to the community's needs or interests is also part of social responsibility. That is plowing back a share of profits for the good of communities.

The four (4) Ps represent the seller's view of the marketing tools available for influencing buyers. From the buyer's point of view, each marketing tool is designed to deliver a customer benefit. It was suggested that the seller's four Ps correspond to the customer's four Cs. The four Cs are customer solution (product), customer cost (price), convenience (place), and communication (promotion).

CHAPTER 9:
CARING FOR YOUR CUSTOMERS

A satisfied customer is the best business strategy of all - Michael LeBoeuf.

So whatever you wish that others would do to you, do also to them, for this is the Law and the Prophets. (Matthew 7:12 ESV).

It is very important to know what your customers need or want and to provide just that. Be honest, even with the quality of goods and services you provide as a business. That will ensure that you always have business.

Advertising and marketing have the same goal in mind: to bring customers in. After that, what happens is up to you. If customers like what they see, if they find great products or service, and if they are treated well, they will return.

When that happens, you have the most prized of all things: a valued, loyal, and returning customer. Experience has shown that it costs five times more to create a new customer than it does to retain a current one. Similarly, there is a rule of thumb that says 80 percent of your business comes from 20 percent of your customers (the 80/20 rule). According to Varga (1997:22), the first and foremost priority of any business owner should be to please the customer. The reason he gives for that is that establishing a long-term relationship with customers is the backbone and lifeblood of your business's survival.

The other thing that will help you stay successful in business is to make new and consistent customers by treating them well, giving them exceptional service, and doing what you say you will do when you say you will do it. Varga (1997:2) further asserts that if it calls for you to go the extra mile to satisfy a customer, do it because that is the best insurance for business success.

On the other hand, you also need to care for your employees. Employees are the backbone of your business. If they are happy, your business runs well; if they are not, well, you know what will happen. Among many jobs, your job once you get your business up and running is to care for these two constituencies. Take care of your customers and employees, and they will take care of you.

Almost every business will have three different types of customers: new customers, existing customers, and exiting customers. You need to know how to handle all three correctly if you want to succeed in business.

New customers

Creating new customers is an ongoing process. It is one of the fun aspects of business. Many entrepreneurs enjoy spending their time figuring out ways to lure in new business.

Many make a mistake after the initial sale. Flush with success, a new entrepreneur often neglects the new customer after that sale, inadvertently failing to realize that that new customer may become one of the valued 20 percent if treated properly.

Turn that new customer into a returning customer by treating him or her well from the start. If you don't, it's the business equivalent of a one-night stand.

Existing customers

Existing customers are one of your most valuable business assets and cannot be taken for granted. They usually make up the bulk of your business, so it is incumbent upon you to nurture that relationship and let those customers know how important they are to you and your business. Existing customers should be given special services and discounts when appropriate, and they should always be shown appreciation for their patronage.

Exiting customers

All businesses will have customers who are ending their relationship for one reason or another. Bear in mind that even these customers need special treatment.

The ending may just be the natural course of the relationship; for example, a customer who is moving away. Because you never know who they talk to or who they may refer to you, this customer needs to be cared for just as well as the others.

Why do customers leave?

1) Some customers leave a business because they have moved away, i.e., have changed locations.
2) Some people change their purchasing habits, meaning they are not buying the same kind of products anymore.
3) Some of the customers decide that they like the competition better.
4) Some customers become angry with a business's overall service.
5) The bulk of them may feel unappreciated, meaning the businessperson does not care about them.

What is the lesson?

Unless you want to lose the bulk of your hard-earned customers, you had better make sure they know that you appreciate their patronage. As old customers leave, you need to constantly be bringing in new customers to take their place. And as you do that, you need to be converting your new customers into existing, loyal customers. This important cycle of your business cannot be ignored. Old customers will leave (because they do), and if there are no new customers coming in to pick up the slack, you will soon be out of business.

What Is Great Customer Service?

Few businesses actually incorporate great customer service into their business operations. It may be because they have never given it much thought, because it is simply not a priority, or because the culture of the company is so hectic that employees feel stressed.

Unless you want to be on a never-ending quest for new customers because you have no returning, loyal ones, you better make customer service a priority. Furthermore, serving your customers well is also a great way to distinguish your business from the competition.

You have to give people a reason to patronize your business.
1) Better prices,
2) A better location
3) Better products,
4) Better service

The essence of superb customer service is that it becomes one of the guiding principles of your business. You need to put pen to paper, create a policy, and then see that every employee receives and understands it. Also, make sure that it is made a part of the employee manual. For employees to realize how important customer service is, it must be stressed every day in many ways.

Great Customer Service

1) Be attentive

Think like a customer. What do they want from you? What are their needs? The better you can meet those needs, the better your customer service.

2) Make it personal.

Endeavour generally to anticipate the needs of particularly special customers. Offer recommendations and ideas that they might be able to use. Become their partner. They won't forget it.

3) Give them a discount.

A discount on future purchases is a great way to make customers feel special and remain loyal.

4) Keep them informed.

Know your customers and call to inform them about any new products or services you have introduced.

5) Take personal responsibility.

Make sure you or your workers act promptly, keep promises, and follow up. The idea is to have one person accept responsibility for fixing a problem, do more than the client expected, and do so in a positive, helpful way.

Conclusion

This is indeed a business manual. It contains all the necessary information you need for starting and managing your business. The size of the business does not matter since the principles have been included. Business is important for any individual who wants to increase his or her finances.

We have explained what entrepreneurship is and what it is all about. That includes its benefits and challenges. Business was explained, along with its main types and forms. Generating business ideas and turning them into opportunities has been discussed. Take advantage of the available opportunities.

A plan is very important. It will help you implement your business ideas. You will know step-by-step what you have to do for your business to make money. People need to be recruited who will make the business function according to expectations. Recruit competent staff, and you will not worry about some things.

No one can know what you are selling unless you make your goods and services known. We call that marketing. This ensures that you provide what the people want at the place and price they can afford. In order to reduce the necessity of getting new customers all the time, take care of your current customers. They are your asset, as they will keep coming back for more purchases if they are satisfied.

Make use of all that you have learned in this business manual. It is not enough to dream of a business. Once you have an idea, arise and start working on it. You will be glad you did. So it is time for you to turn your dreams into reality. You now have the necessary information. Take action.

BIBLIOGRAPHY

SCARBOROUGH, N. M., (2012) Effective Small Business Management- An Entrepreneurial Approach. Tenth Edition. New Jersey: Prentice Hall.

ANONYMOUS, (2016). Small Business Defined. Available at http://www.yourdictionary.com/small-business. Accessed [Online] on 14th December 2016.

HOLT, D. D. (2002). Entrepreneurship New Venture Creation. New Delhi: Prentice Hall.

ZIMMERER, T. W. and SCARBOROUGH, N. M. (20015). Essentials of Entrepreneurship and Small Business Management. 4th edition. New Delhi: Prentice Hall.

THOMPSON, A. A., STRICKLAND, A. J. III, PETERAF, M. A., JANES, A., GAMBLE, J.E., SUTTON, C. (2013). Crafting and Executing Strategy The Quest for Competitive Advantage- Concepts and Cases. European Edition. New York: McGraw- Hill Education.

THOMPSON, A. A., Jr., STRICKLAND, A. J. III, and GAMBLE J.E., (2007). Crafting and Executing Strategy - Concepts and Cases. 15th Edition. Boston: Irwin McGraw- Hill.

SHER, B., (2000). What Rich People Know & Desperately Want to keep Secret. 1st Edition. Nigeria: Self-Improvement Publishing.

FIRER, C., ROSS, S., WESTERFIELD, R. W., JORDAN, B. D. (2012). Fundamentals of Corporate Finance. 05th South African edition. UK: McGraw Hill education.

KOTLER, P., KELLER, K. L., (2016). Marketing Management. 15th Global Edition. USA: Pearson Education Inc.

VARGA, K. J., (1997). How to get customers to call, buy & beg for more! 1st edition. USA: World Wide Publishing & Trading International, LLC.

ANONYMOUS, (2017). What is business? Available at http://www.businessdictionary.com/. Accessed [Online] on 09th March 2017.

ANONYMOUS, (2017). What is a business? Available at http://www.investopedia.com/. Accessed [Online] on 09th March 2017.

DYSON, J. R. (2010). Accounting for Non- Accounting Students. 08th Edition. England: Pearson Education Limited.

ANONYMOUS, (2017). What is manufacturing business. Available at http://study.com/academy. Accessed [Online] on 10th March 2017.

ANONYMOUS, (2017). Wholesaling. Available at http://www.investopedia.com. Accessed [Online] on 10th March 2017.

MARTINS, A. T. (2017). Business Ideas vs. Opportunities: What is the Difference? Available at http://www.mytopbusinessideas.com/ideas-vs-opportunities. Accessed [Online] on 10th March 2017.

CISP, (2014). Income generating activities and support to small enterprises. Available at www.cisp-som.org. Accessed [Online] on 11th March 2014.

BRUNINGS, J., (2017). Differences between Business plan and Strategic plan. Available at https://onstrategyhq.com/resources/what-is-the-difference-between-a-business-plan-and-a-strategic-plan/. Accessed [Online] on 14th March 2017.

WIKIPEDIA, (2017). Strategic planning. Available at https://en.wikipedia.org/wiki/Strategic_planning. Accessed [Online] on 14th March 2017.

BERRY, T. (2017). What is a Business Plan? Available at http://articles.bplans.com/what-is-a-business-plan/. Accessed [Online] on 14th March 2017.

MAITAH, I. M. (2017). How Culture Affects your Business.

Available at www.maitah.com. Accessed [Online] on 23rd March 2017.

IAC Publishing, (2017). How Competitors affect business activity. Available at https://www.reference.com/business-finance. Accessed [Online] on 23rd March 2017.

REGENT Business School, (2007). Marketing Management Module Guide. RSA: REGENT Business School.

About the Author

He was born in the Kingdom of Swaziland. He is the Managing Director of Life Solutions Investments (Pty) Ltd. Furthermore, he is the founder and Pastor of Freedom Centre International Church in Swaziland. He believes that freedom in life is everyone's portion and that such is possible by choice.

Mdluli is currently on the final stage of his Master of Business Administration (MBA) with REGENT Business School. He also studied ministry and theology in Calvary University. Before then, he studied Bachelor of Commerce at the University of Swaziland. He is the former General Manager of a Savings and Credit Co-operative.

OTHER BOOKS BY
THE AUTHOR

1. The Secrets of Successful Marriage and True Love! Find Out What You've Been Missing
2. Explosive Secrets that Guarantee Prayer Results You Can Be Proud of
3. Winning Every Spiritual Battle in Half the Time

CONNECT WITH THE AUTHOR

Thank you for reading my book! Here are my social media coordinates, website and blogs:

Friend me on Facebook: http://facebook.com/elphas.mdluli
Follow me on Twitter: http://twitter.com/Inforsipho
Subscribe to my blog: https://freedomhub.biz/blog-4/
Other blog: https://singlesandcouplescoach.wordpress.com/
Connect on LinkedIn: https://www.linkedin.com/in/elphas-mdluli/
TikTok: https://www.tiktok.com/@esmdluli

www.ingramcontent.com/pod-product-compliance
Lightning Source LLC
Chambersburg PA
CBHW051324220526
45468CB00004B/1486